Art from scrap materials

ART FROM SCRAP MATERIALS
Robin Capon

B T Batsford Limited

London and Sydney

Designed by Libra Studios
Filmset in 11/12½ pt Monophoto Bembo by
Servis Filmsetting Limited, Manchester
for the publishers
B T Batsford Limited
4 Fitzhardinge Street, London W1H 0AH
23 Cross Street, Brookvale, NSW 2100, Australia

Reproduced and printed by photolithography and bound in
Great Britain at The Pitman Press, Bath

Contents

Acknowledgment

I wish to thank all those who have allowed me to use their work in this book. I am especially grateful to the Trustees of the Tate Gallery, London, for granting permission to reproduce works in their collection. I am also indebted to Mr Neville Barrow, teacher of metal sculpture at Gateway School, Leicester, and his pupils, for the metal sculptures, and to John Nowell for the photography of that work. My thanks are also due to Miss Thelma M Nye and Miss Harriet Murray-Browne, my editors, for their advice on the compilation of this book, and to my wife, Patricia, for typing the manuscript.

1 Introduction

In an age when craft shops and suppliers offer an extensive range of art equipment it is not surprising that the idea of creative work with scrap and waste materials is often overlooked. Indeed, many conventional, mass-produced art materials, used with imagination, give interesting and satisfying results. However, not all schools or individuals have the financial resources to stock these, especially in the quantity normally required for a large class; moreover, modern equipment and materials do not, of course, guarantee good results if interest and stimuli are lacking. There is a place then, at all levels of art education, for art from scrap materials.

Scrap offers exciting possibilities for a whole range of art work. Much of the litter which we daily discard without a second thought can be useful. Cartons, paper and cardboard used for packaging, offcuts of paper, lengths of string and thread, and pieces of fabric, for example, may have tremendous potential for use in collage, appliqué, assemblages, low relief and other forms of design. Similarly, there is a wealth of suitable articles in dustbins, waste-paper baskets, rubbish-tips and junk yards to employ in constructions and sculpture. 'Found' materials and products of nature, whether from shoreline, wood or field, can also be used.

1 Juan Gris, *The Sunblind*
The Tate Gallery, London
Copyright by A.D.A.G.P. Paris, 1974

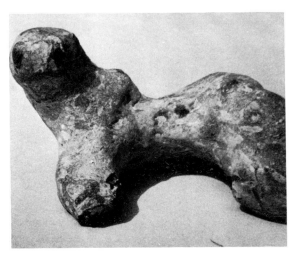

2 A flint

Normally we accept all this just as rubbish and far too readily overlook it as a source of inspiration or for direct use in art work. But scrap materials have been used by well-known artists: cuttings from newspapers, tickets and other items were incorporated into Cubist pictures as long ago as 1912. *The Sunblind* by Juan Gris, figure 1 illustrates this. At the same time, Georges Braque was bringing typeset phrases and strips of wallpaper into his paintings. The intention of these artists was to introduce a reality of substance and texture, perhaps contrasting this with textures expressed in paint. Later the Futurists, Dadaists and Surrealists used scrap materials and found objects in their work. Boccioni's *Fusion of a Head and Window*, which is formed from a plaster head with locks of real hair, and a window-frame, is an early example of assemblage. The collages of Kurt Schwitters achieve a poetic quality and dignity from such modest materials as discarded papers, wrappings and bus-tickets. In recent times 'Pop' artists have employed similar techniques.

The scrap of the man-made and natural world can likewise *suggest* many ideas for art work, just as the bicycle saddle and handle-bars suggested a bull's head to Picasso. Scrap materials may stimulate ideas; it is not essential actually to use them in the production or construction of the work. A

3 Henry Moore, *Recumbent Figure*
The Tate Gallery, London

flint found on one of the beaches of North Kent, figure 2, instantly reminded me of the sculpture of Henry Moore. The link is a valid one, for much of Moore's work is evolved from the study of such natural forms. Although most of the examples illustrated in this book were made from waste materials, the use of these as inspiration for traditional methods of working should not be neglected. And of course scrap can be used for the actual execution of work. Lengths of card and oddments of fabric, for example, can replace brushes for painting.

The aim of this book, therefore, is to promote the adventurous use of such materials; to encourage an awareness of scrap as well as to illustrate ways in which it might be used, and to suggest ideas for further work and exploration. With the experience of 'new' materials and fresh ideas and techniques this work will test imagination and ingenuity. I hope that these ideas will encourage a more creative and adventurous approach to design and three-dimensional work.

Sometimes the material itself will suggest a method of design; alternatively it may be selected because it is especially suitable for portraying a particular subject: for example, in figure 4, the buttons used as eyes and the lengths of drinking

4 Collage from fabric and found materials: girl aged four

straws for legs. Other inspiration for art with scrap materials might be the work of modern artists or 'forms' in nature.

It will be necessary to collect material over a period of time, though it is surprising how quickly it will accumulate. Although it is not essential to have a vast reserve to draw upon, it is obvious that, in some circumstances, a variety of materials will be required. This type of work can easily be carried out at school, provided there is an organised approach and adequate room for storage. Apart from the scrap, only the basic art room or studio equipment is necessary.

A book which attempts to cover such a wide variety of work must, of necessity, be selective. Thus, in the main, I have kept to common waste materials which will be readily available to most people. The illustrations range from the work of young children to that of eminent artists; most of the ideas described are adaptable to all levels of ability. By employing various simple techniques the materials can be used to create work of great variety and interest. Many of the techniques can be elaborated upon once the basic idea has been understood, and it is hoped therefore that the reader will not merely imitate what he sees on the following pages, but rather be inspired to create fresh and original ideas from his own particular scrap.

2 The materials

The most commonplace materials can be useful, though obviously it is not a practical proposition to hoard everything. Collecting for 'scrap art' is an important process in itself. Some materials are extremely versatile and worthy of a place in everyone's collection. Waste paper, for example, is suitable for a range of techniques in both two and three dimensions. A collection may be governed by specific projects which are to be carried out, or it may be made up of a whole variety of interesting scrap which could be useful in time. Either way, and particularly with the help of others, it should not take long to accumulate an interesting and sufficiently large stock. Common items of scrap are shown in figure 5. Storage should be organised according to the method and the type of work to be undertaken.

Low relief techniques will involve mainly cutting or tearing, and gluing. A large variety of papers, as well as other materials which can be glued to a support of paper, card or board, is therefore desirable. All types of paper offcuts can be saved for this purpose, including the trimmed edges of paintings, prints and photographs. Scraps of textured and embossed paper can be used, and those which are transparent or semi-transparent can be particularly interesting. Newspapers, magazines, old books and posters provide another source of material. Any discarded paper in the form of wrappers, packets, tickets, check–out slips, receipts, stamps, envelopes, foil tops and labels, is useful. Pieces of aluminium foil, corrugated paper, wallpaper and sandpaper can also be employed in

5   A selection of useful materials

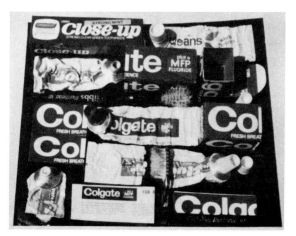

6   Assemblage from used tubes and packets

7 Stapled construction using cardboard tubes

8 Cartons and string

such work. It is impossible here to list all the many papers which are available; suffice it to say that although a large array of materials is not essential to good work, variety is often a stimulus. What is important is that the materials available are put to some imaginative use.

Other scrap may have potential for relief work. Provided that the correct glue is used, there are many other scrap objects which can be attached to a support to form a design. Such materials will include empty tins, cotton-reels, match boxes, cartons and canisters, bottle tops, wood shavings and offcuts of various types of wood. Figure 6 is an assemblage made from this type of scrap. Here, glue was not used; instead the objects were pressed into a coating of quick-drying PVA paint.

With much of the work suggested in this book, unlimited choice can lead to confusion and in turn poor results. Collage, for example, can easily become nothing more than playing around with various materials. The results may be interesting and unusual, but go no more. It is always necessary to create some kind of relationship between one item or shape and the next. This can be done in both a mental and a visual way. In figure 6 the design is visually satisfying and at the same time there is a mental association of the various parts because they are all connected with toothpaste. This illustration also demonstrates that quite ordinary waste materials can become more exciting if they are cut up or cut open in some way.

Appliqué and collage work can make use of all

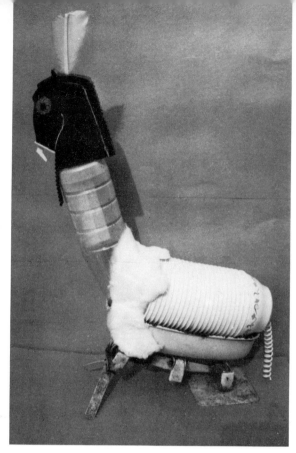

9 Various materials

kinds of fabric remnants: upholstery scraps, old stockings, lace, printed fabrics, leather, towelling, PVC, nylon and hessian (burlap). String, wool and thread are also useful. Shells, pebbles and chips of stone, coloured glass or china can be embedded in wet PVA paint, plaster or *Polyfilla* (*Spackle*).

With sculpture and construction work one can add all sorts of other junk to the list. Usually it is necessary to make use of what is locally available, though for the completion of a design one or two specific items may have to be found. It has been mentioned that some objects suggest a particular interpretation. The work of children is often motivated in this way, by seeing in the materials shapes which they associate with objects and beings in their everyday life.

Apart from cardboard and wood, useful junk for sculpture may include bits of plastic, polystyrene, tin and heavy fabric, in addition to wire and wire mesh, tins, bottles, coat hangers, discarded saucepans, toys, old bicycle wheels, and pieces from old engines, television sets, radios and other domestic appliances. Figures 7 to 9 are simple examples of three-dimensional work with common waste materials. The cardboard tubes in figure 7 were stapled together. An old pair of scales serves as the base for the animal in figure 9, which also makes use of plastic containers, cotton wool, a bottle, an old moneybox, a feather, a cork and a drawing pin. It is possible to exploit the natural texture or appearance of the materials used in such models, though they can also be brush or spray painted.

Sources of materials

Some sources have already been implied. It is obvious from the various lists in the previous chapter that objects which we would normally term as litter or rubbish can in fact be put to use, and therefore instead of throwing them into the dustbin they can be added to the store of useful scrap. Local shops and factories may provide another source. Shops often discard packaging materials, which can be of great variety in shape, colouring and texture, and may be of paper, cardboard, plastic, polystyrene or wood. For school work, where a large quantity may be required, this can be a particularly useful source. Offcuts of various materials may be obtainable from factories, whilst a local wood-yard or builder's will give away odd bits and pieces of timber. Building sites, scrap merchants and rubbish-tips are other useful sources of scrap. A printer may be willing to dispose of trimmed offcuts of various papers.

Materials taken from natural sources may exhibit qualities not found in most of the scrap previously mentioned. In a seaside town one could make use of driftwood, shells, pebbles and so on. Leaves, dried grasses, straw, seeds, feathers, eggshells, animal fur and hair, and bark will be available in the country. In some areas it may be possible to find lumps of chalk or stone for carving.

Although every home produces its own supply of scrap, it is worthwhile investigating one or two of these other sources for unusual new materials.

Storage

The amount of space available for storage may well determine what sort of work is undertaken. Space is not only required for storage of the various scrap materials, it is also needed for the work whilst under construction and when completed. Indeed, in the modern art room this may prove to be quite a problem, and is obviously something which must be carefully considered before embarking on any work. A shed or old workshop is the ideal location for junk sculpture.

As to the storage of the materials, some kind of system must be devised in order to save time and prevent frustration when looking for particular items. Materials can often be stored in large, strong cardboard boxes, the contents of which are clearly labelled on the outside. One box, for example, might contain tins, another fabric remnants, another paper offcuts, and so on. It is as well to ensure that adequate materials are available before the work begins.

Organisation of work

Whether in the studio or the school art room, it is essential to approach the work in an organised and disciplined way. The working space should be of a reasonable size, and the scrap materials and any others which are necessary should be readily available. There must be space for work to be stored and left to dry.

Organisation is especially important in the classroom, where it may be advantageous, particularly when working with large groups, to work on a step-by-step basis. This, obviously, does not preclude originality and creativity in the work.

Additional equipment

Although the work involves mainly scrap materials it is, of course, occasionally necessary to combine these with conventional art materials. Further, a particular technique may require the use of certain materials and equipment. Where this is so there is adequate explanation in the text.

In general, scissors, brushes, craft knives, rollers, pliers, a hammer, a saw, wire-cutters, as well as glues, paints, inks and varnishes will cover additional equipment.

Methods of painting and other finish techniques are described in the notes at the back of the book.

3 Paper and cardboard

Paper and cardboard are the commonest of waste materials and may be employed in many different ways. These are ideal materials when space and facilities are limited. Used imaginatively different papers can produce an immense variety of results.

Collage

The term 'collage' may be defined as picture building by pasting cut or torn shapes on to a support. Any waste material which can be glued to a support is suitable, and the enthusiastic collagist will be constantly looking for interesting materials with which to work. Art papers can be supplemented with labels, tickets, check-out slips, stamps, playing cards, corrugated paper, foil paper, photographs, negatives, scraps of wallpaper, as well as fabric remnants, matchsticks, lids, seeds, string and so on.

Cut-paper and collage work can be adapted to all levels of ability. With this type of work one must always be prepared to reject or amend ideas in the process of making something visually interesting and satisfying.

10 Extended design made from a collage of sweet
wrappings

11 Division into strips

12 Cutting and rebuilding

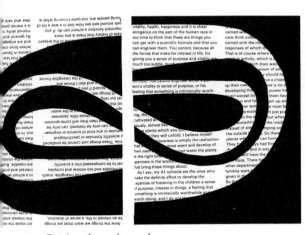

13 Cutting through two layers

The extended design shown in figure 10 was cut from a sheet of paper which had been covered with various sweet labels and wrappings. Nothing was added or taken away, the parts being slightly spaced out before being glued to another sheet of paper.

Papers which differ in tone, colour, texture and thickness, will give variety and interest to the work. The colour pages of supplements and magazines are useful. Most work which could be done with manufactured art papers can be done just as effectively with scrap paper. There is not room here to describe all these different techniques; books on particular subjects, such as collage, will elaborate on the techniques which are possible. The basic necessities for this work are a pair of sharp scissors, a good paper glue (*Polycell* or *Gloy*, with PVA medium for heavier papers and cardboard), a glue brush and a support of paper or card on which to work.

Simple but effective results are possible using the techniques of division, extended design, cutting and rebuilding, folding and silhouettes. An extended design from scrap papers has been illustrated in figure 10. Spacing plays a vital part in these designs and nothing should be added to or subtracted from the basic shape. Old photographs and pictures cut from magazines are ideal for exercises based on division, as in figure 11. The parts can be replaced in the same order, as in the example, to give the 'broken image' effect, or they can be reassembled in a different order. In figure 12 the various parts originated from a number of

14 Silhouette made from folded paper

16 Pattern made from shapes cut from folded paper

15 Silhouette made by cutting shapes from a square

17 Silhouettes

circles. Alternatively, if a number of identical shapes are cut from a picture, these can be replaced in a different order. Shapes can also be cut from two (or more) sheets of paper at once, as in figure 13, with the rebuilt design employing shapes from each layer. Using folded paper is a quick way of producing shapes for pattern work, see figure 16. Silhouettes can also be cut from folded paper (figure 14), from several layers at once (figure 17), a method which is particularly suitable for freizes, or simply by cutting in from the edges of a shape (figure 15). A great many variations are possible with each of these techniques and they can all make use of oddments of paper left over from other work, offcuts, and waste papers.

Holiday souvenirs form the collage in figure 18. Here the idea of association is exploited: all the papers were collected whilst on holiday and are therefore linked by this fact. Relationships of shape, colour, and texture remain important.

Other materials may be combined with paper to build the collage. Examples of fabric collage are shown in figures 49 to 51. Techniques such as froissage (wrinkling), décollage (tearing away), brûlage (burning) and fumage (toning with smoke) can be employed. Collage can be over-worked with graphic techniques; its directness of approach and the physical contact with materials gives it an important place in art teaching.

18 Collage: *Holiday Souvenirs*

Paper mosaic

Paper mosaic is a technique which will require a reserve of various colours and textures. Small pieces of paper of about 12 mm ($\frac{1}{2}$ in.) square are used to build up the design, as in figures 19 and 20. These pictures were made by children aged six and seven respectively, showing what a lively medium paper can be; in both, papers cut from magazines and supplements were used. The design should be bold and may be sketched in first. Methods of working vary but it is normally best to start with the main shape and then to work outwards, filling in the background. Inspiration for themes might come from the study of actual mosaic work and visits to local examples. It is quickest to cut strips of paper about 12 mm ($\frac{1}{2}$ in.) wide and then to cut these into roughly square shapes. Apply glue to the backing paper and press the small squares into place. This is a good technique for group work.

19 Mosaic collage: girl aged six

20 Mosaic collage: girl aged seven

Assemblage

Assemblage involves the collecting and assembling of material on to a support in collage form, and generally entails working in relief. In figure 21 paper cylinders of various sizes have been glued to a painted hardboard base. The cylinders were made by coiling lengths of paper around a short piece of dowel, overlapping the ends and gluing them together. Impact adhesive, thick PVA medium or perhaps PVA paint (see figure 22) should be used for this heavier three-dimensional work. Figure 21 suggests similar work with tins or cardboard tubing. See also figure 6. Offcuts of wood and perspex (plexiglas), cartons and other scrap can be used in the same way.

21 Assemblage: paper offcuts

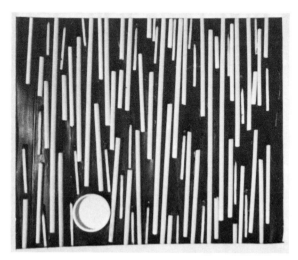

22 Collage: drinking straws, match sticks, ice lolly sticks

Rubbings

Anything in low relief will give a rubbing and scrap items such as leaves and feathers provide interesting surfaces. Rubbings can be made with heelball, wax crayon, Conté, chalk or a soft pencil, on newsprint, cartridge paper (drawing paper) or other coloured papers. Experiments will decide which combination of tool and paper is the best, though wax on newsprint is generally successful. The wax crayon is used on its side with pressure applied gradually so as to build up a good, positive result. Different rubbings can be superimposed over one another, or the rubbing used with other graphic and collage work. Figure 23 shows a rubbing which was taken from the extended design illustrated in figure 10.

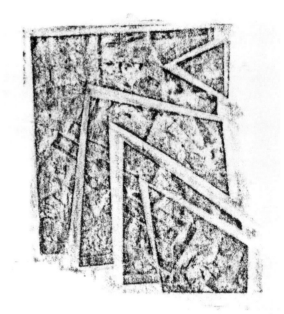

23 Rubbing from figure 10

Printmaking

Waste paper and cardboard will give a surprising variety of results with simple printmaking techniques. Basically all the equipment required here is a roller, printing ink and the waste materials. Again, it may be necessary to consult books dealing specifically with printing to gain a full knowledge and understanding of the techniques.

Water-based printing ink is recommended as it is easier to clean up after use. A bed of ink, made by rolling ink evenly over a zinc plate, tin lid or piece of formica or glass, will provide the foundation for many simple prints. The ink can be scraped away with a piece of cardboard or masked out with cut or torn shapes. It is then covered with a sheet of printing paper, and the print is taken by rolling over or burnishing the back of this. Torn paper shapes were used in figure 24. When the paper shapes are removed, a further print may be taken, as in figure 25. Both scraping into the ink and masking were used in figure 26. The circle is a cork print.

In figure 27 a small cardboard tube was used to create a printed pattern. A piece of dowel dipped in ink was used in figure 28, this time on newspaper. Other items of scrap, a screwed-up piece of paper or a section cut from an egg-box for example, can be used in this way.

24 Paper resist print: positive

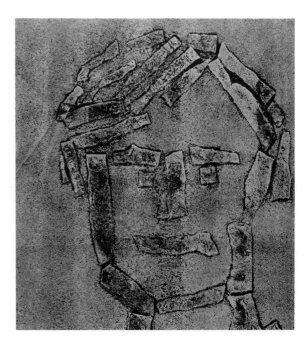

25 Paper resist print: negative

Prints can also be taken from leaves and other textured surfaces. String, wood-wool (used for packing) and foil tops are among other materials which can be pressed into a bed of ink before taking a print. Prints can be made from paper shapes or from blocks formed by gluing various types of paper and cardboard to a cardboard base. Such blocks are easily assembled, the prints are produced quickly, and this method does not necessitate the complex processes of many other forms of block printing. A variety of techniques are involved: cutting, gluing, and printing. The method serves as a useful introduction to print making and is recommended for classwork. Cardboard blocks of about 255 mm × 205 mm (10 in. × 8 in.) are best, using a strong glue for attaching shapes to the base and a small roller for inking. The character of these prints is determined to a large extent by the materials used, and the amount of relief and spacing, see figure 29.

Other prints can be made by cutting or impressing a design into a soft surface; scraps of clay or polystyrene, for example.

Figure 30 is a drawing using a small length of corrugated cardboard dipped in indian ink.

26 Monoprint: masking and scraping techniques

27 Print made from a cardboard tube

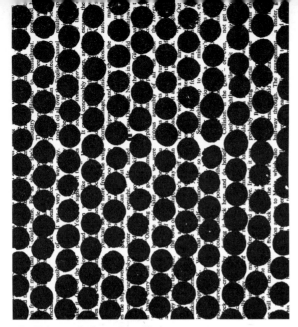

28 Print made from dowelling on newspaper

30 Drawing made with a length of
corrugated cardboard dipped in ink

29 Block print: various materials

Using masks and templates

Masking with shapes cut from waste paper can also be employed in pictorial and design work. In figure 31 the thin powder paint was applied with a spray diffuser. The paper mask has been used in a number of positions. Each time the paper was sprayed with a different colour before the mask was moved. The mask must be left in place until the paint has dried, otherwise there is a risk of smearing the work. Masking may also be used with flicked paint and aerosol spray paint.

Similarly, cut pieces of cardboard can be used as templates. In figure 32 the template was drawn round in various positions and the resultant shapes then painted in, using a limited colour range.

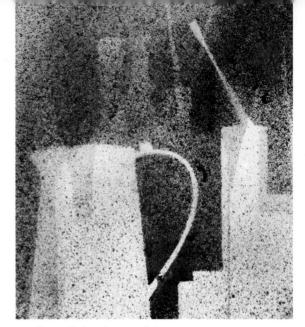

31 Spray design: boy aged sixteen

32 Template design: boy aged thirteen

33 Folded paper

Three-dimensional work

Work with paper and cardboard can include many simple three-dimensional techniques. All the examples shown on the following pages are suitable for class teaching; most of them involve paper or card offcuts, corrugated cardboard or cardboard boxes.

Free-standing work using folding, bending and slotting techniques is illustrated in figures 33 to 37. These methods can be used to create three-dimensional forms without employing glue, staples or other fixing aids. Cardboard can be scored with a sharp knife and folded back, whilst individually folded units can be interlocked or attached by other methods to create more complex structures. The work can be further developed by cutting out shapes along some of the folds, by using a paper punch, or by gluing on shapes. Folded paper, as in figure 33, could therefore be used merely as the basic structure of three-dimensional work.

Bending and coiling will also create shapes which are self-supporting. Tin and wire, as well as paper and card, are suitable materials for this. If rolled around tubing, dowel or pencils, the paper can then be allowed to unravel to the desired extent, as in figure 34. In figure 35 a roll of newspaper has been cut at intervals to approximately half its length before being partially pulled up from the centre.

Slotting techniques are shown in figures 36 and 37, and again in figure 41. There are two basic methods: shapes can be inserted into slots which have been made in the main form (see figure 41),

34 Coiled card

35 Rolled newspaper

36 Slotted card

or slots made in each shape can be used as an interlocking device (see figure 37). Drinking straws, as in figure 40, can be joined by inserting small lengths of pipe-cleaners, and can be pushed into holes which have been punched into tins or cardboard. Slots can be cut with a craft knife, razor blade or scissors; the first two can be extremely dangerous and are not recommended for use by children.

For the model in figure 38 coiling, folding, bending and slotting techniques were employed; glue was only used for attaching the eye, a melon seed. The model was made by adding paper shapes to the basic cardboard tube, as was the grasshopper illustrated in figure 39. Here the painted card shapes have been stapled on and the hind legs fixed by paper fasteners.

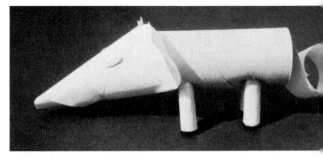

38 Starting from a tube

39 Building around a tube

37 Slotting

34

Mobiles

A mobile can be another effective way of using scrap material. Cut-outs from cardboard or paper which have been painted or decorated in collage form can be suspended with thread from a wire frame. In figure 40 the flower shapes were suspended from a coat-hanger.

40 Mobile

Models from folded cardboard

The model in figure 41 was made from a folded piece of corrugated cardboard with identical shapes cut from either side of the fold, as shown in the diagram, figure 42, where the black lines represent cuts. The shaded areas were discarded. The shapes left between the legs were used as wings, being slotted into the body. The model is balanced and free-standing.

41 Folded corrugated cardboard

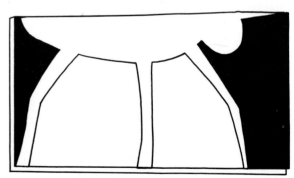

42 Diagram of insect

Pop-up models

'Pop-up' models can be made from cut and folded paper or from cut and scored cardboard. The basic shape should be simple so that it is easy to cut out, and the base must be sufficiently wide enough to support the weight of the shape above it. Models cut from heavy cardboard may need additional support in the form of a folded piece of card glued to the back. Figure 43 shows the shape cut out from its cardboard surround joined only at the base, which is a straight line. In figure 44 the shape has been pushed forward so as to stand vertically to the surround. Feathers, torn newspaper and fabric are used to decorate the surface of the shape.

43 'Pop-up' model, shape in place

44 'Pop-up' model

Other ideas

Cardboard is also used in figures 45 and 46. Figure 45 is supported by scoring the cardboard to make a fold, whilst figure 46 is slotted into a cardboard tube.

Various odd scraps of paper were cut and used to create the face illustrated in figure 47. The basic shape is a cylinder made from thin card.

Paper may, of course, be combined with other materials to make models and constructions. In figure 48 the basic shape is a perfume container with a screw-top. Holes were made to insert the whiskers and the tail, whilst the paper ears were glued at the join between container and screw-top. This is another instance where the scrap material itself suggested a particular interpretation.

45 Folded cardboard

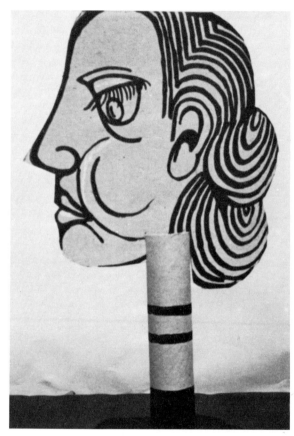

46 Slotted cardboard

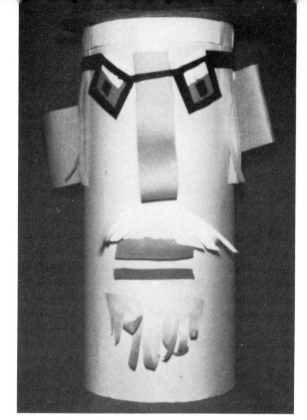

47 Cardboard model

48 Model made from various materials

4 Fabric and string

Appliqué and collage work can make use of all kinds of fabric remnants: upholstery scraps, old stockings, lace, printed fabrics, leather, towelling, PVC, nylon and hessian (burlap) are among those which are useful.

Fabric collage and appliqué

Fabrics can be cut or torn and glued to a support to form a collage. With appliqué, as in figure 53, the shapes are sewn on. The techniques of sewing and gluing could be combined.

Many of the techniques described for paper collage can be adapted for use with fabric. Fabrics vary in their quality and texture. Some, for example organdie, are semi-transparent and one can exploit this in the collage. Others will fray when cut, and again this quality can be used effectively. Careful selection is important, and a satisfying relationship between the various fabric parts should be the objective.

Most fabrics are easily cut with a pair of sharp scissors or pinking shears. The shapes may be overlapped or superimposed and are simply glued to a support of paper, card, board or fabric. A quick-drying, non-staining glue is recommended, such as PVA Medium or *Copydex*. These two will stick all the fabrics listed above. Paper glues are usually unsuitable. It is unnecessary to coat the whole of the fabric shape with glue, instead just apply it to the edges. Sometimes just a few spots will suffice.

With fabric collage it is best to arrange all the parts on the support before gluing, so that it is possible to make alterations to the design. It is easier to work on a foundation background consisting of two or three bold strips of fabric rather than to have to cut a shape to fit exactly in to those which surround it. The former method really amounts to a selection of silhouettes, perhaps overlapped, glued to a simple background. This is

49 Fabric collage: boy aged five

51 Fabric collage: girl aged six

50 Fabric collage: girl aged seven

52 Cutting through several layers: fabric and paper

illustrated in figures 49 and 50. These examples, together with figure 51 illustrate the potential of this technique with small children. The children are able to achieve more defined forms than they could with paint and therefore the results are possibly more satisfying. With older children pure fabric collage may become more suited to girls, but, of course, fabric can be combined with paper and other materials. Wool has been used in figure 51 whilst in figure 52 fabric is combined with various types of paper. This collage was made by cutting through several layers of paper and fabric at once, and then using parts from each layer to build the design.

53 Appliqué

Designing with string

String, wool and thread can be used in exactly the same way as other collage materials. String has been combined with lace and other materials in figure 54. Various lengths, thicknesses, types and colours can be used and the frayed edge exploited. A design with string is illustrated in figure 55.

Prints and rubbings can be taken from blocks made by gluing string to a cardboard base. Impressed into a bed of ink, string can be used to make monoprints, as described on page 28.

54 Collage: lace, string, match sticks and paper

55 String design: string impressed into PVA paint

43

Three-dimensional work with string

In three-dimensional work, wool, string, twine and thread, also wire and raffia, are useful for binding separate parts of a model together. Different types, or variations in thickness and colour, add to the interest of the work. Thread may also be used to suspend shapes, either individually, or as integrated parts of a mobile. A variety of free-standing work can be made from a basic structure of twisted newspaper or cardboard tubing which is then bound and strengthened with wool, string or raffia. If the wool is applied in two layers, each made in a different direction, then this will add strength to the work. Fabric offcuts can be wrapped around the shapes before they are bound together. Ends must be firmly tied and neatly finished.

Simple models can be made from a single length of wire (perhaps an old coat-hanger), which is twisted and bent into shape. In figures 56 and 57 the armatures were made from pipe cleaners. These were covered with discarded lengths of wool, and other details were sewn on. Pieces of fabric may be combined with other materials, as shown in figure 58. This model, built around a bottle, is made of fabric and paper shapes, a spent light bulb for the head, and seeds for the eyes.

56 Pipe cleaners, wool, fabric: girl aged six

44

57 Pipe cleaners, wool, fabric: girl aged six

58 Fabric and various materials

5 Wood

The purpose of this section is to suggest and illustrate ways in which wood can be used for creative work. It is important to understand the material being used, to appreciate the various kinds of wood and the ways these respond to different treatment, to exploit surfaces, textures and so on. Most of the work in the following illustrations was made from scrap wood, using basic techniques and common tools.

Suitable wood includes packing material, shavings, wooden crates and boxes, offcuts from builders' merchants or carpenters, logs and driftwood. The choice of wood for a particular project will be determined by the technique to be used and the effect required. Decayed wood must be avoided. The wood should be dry and it is advisable for children and beginners to keep to softwoods, as these are easier to cut. Basic tools are a tenon saw, a hammer, a chisel and a rasp. Holes can be drilled with a brace and bit, a hand drill or an electric drill. Final smoothing and polishing is done with a file and sandpaper. A vice and a workbench can be useful. Those inexperienced in handling such tools must, of course, be given clear instructions, as tools which are mishandled are obviously potentially dangerous. Young children should not be allowed to operate electrical equipment.

It is normally necessary to make clean, perhaps precise, cuts through a block of wood. Children may need practice at this; they will also discover that wood tends to split if nailed across the grain. Indeed, wood requires more discipline in its working than almost any other substance.

Building with strips of wood

Building with wooden strips is a useful way to start. A strip of wood is cut into sections or alternatively a selection of offcuts is used. One can make use of various widths, lengths and thicknesses. The sawn edges should be clean and square and will need sandpapering to obtain a smooth finish. The aim is to build a free-standing structure by gluing the sections together with some kind of quick-drying glue. *Evo-stick* or another impact adhesive is recommended.

In figure 59 strips of 50 mm × 25 mm (2 in. × 1 in.) softwood have been used, each trimmed to a different length. Experiments will reveal a whole range of possibilities. Colour could be introduced.

In figure 60 a sawn log has been used. Here the individual sections were kept in their correct sequence, only moved slightly from their original positions before being glued. Balance is an important factor in this particular example. Once more, variations will be obvious: one could, for example, arrange the sections in a different order, or mount them on a plywood base to form a relief design. Similar work is possible with dowel offcuts and other round-section wood, such as broom handles. Always aim at neat work with sandpapered edges and careful gluing. If the result is to be varnished or have additional work done to it, ensure that the glue has thoroughly dried before this is done.

59 Assembled wooden offcuts

60 A log, cut and rebuilt

Relief work

An example of relief work is illustrated in Joe Tilson's *Wood Relief, No 17* (figure 61). This work shows how slight variations of surface can effect a design which is visually powerful and interesting. In this example the grain and texture of the individual wooden blocks is also important.

Layering

Another way of producing three-dimensional shapes is by layering. Layers of wood are glued one on top of the other to form a rough, basic shape, which is then worked over with a rasp, surform plane, file and sandpaper until the desired form emerges. This method enables different thicknesses and types of wood to be used which can create a variety of surfaces and colours in the design.

61 Joe Tilson, *Wood Relief No 17*
The Tate Gallery, London

Drilled wood

Tools which can be used to make holes of various sizes in a board have already been mentioned. Centre-bits will prove to be the most useful, whilst a countersink can be used to create impressions in the surface of the wood without actually drilling right through. A board which has had holes drilled in it could then be cut into strips in such a way so that the line of some of the cuts passes through the centre of the holes. The strips can then be arranged so as to align the semicircular cuts in various ways, creating new relationships as part of a single free-standing design. These parts are glued together with an impact adhesive. Blocks which have been drilled can, of course, be combined with those which have not. Some blocks could be painted and a result could be achieved similar to that of Barbara Hepworth's *Square with two Circles*, (even though this is made of metal, figure 62). Wooden shapes can be linked together by inserting a length of dowel through drilled holes. The dowel must be the same size as the holes. Plywood strips can also be slotted together, as with the cardboard example on page 34.

62 Barbara Hepworth, *Square with two Circles*, The Tate Gallery, London

Combining wood with other materials

Strips of wood, such as balsa wood, can be combined with shapes cut from paper, card, cardboard, perspex (plexiglas), celluloid and other materials to create three-dimensional constructions. Use balsa cement or a similar glue to attach shapes to the wood. In figure 64 polystyrene shapes have been used, also caps from various bottles.

Materials may be combined in other ways. In figure 66 wood shavings have been used for the eyes.

63   Match sticks and allied materials: boy aged fifteen

64   Balsa, polystyrene and lids

65 Offcuts, bolts and washers

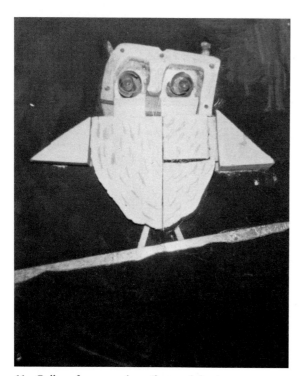

66 Collage from wooden offcuts and shavings

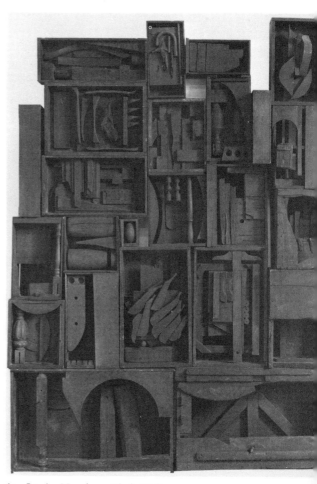

67 Louise Nevelson, *Black Wall 1959*
The Tate Gallery, London

Silhouettes

Silhouettes, as in figure 68, can be cut from ply-wood, timber waste or driftwood, with a fretsaw, bow saw or tenon saw. The fish has been painted and decorated with collage and the eye is a drawing pin. Driftwood is normally soft and easily carved with a penknife. Silhouettes may be free-standing as in figure 68, or they may be mounted as a relief design on a base board of plywood, hardboard or composition board.

68 Decorated silhouette

Log sculpture

A log sculpture can be made with a log which has been shaped with a chisel, or it can simply be an interesting 'found' piece of wood which is cut to the desired shape, smoothed in places with a rasp or sandpaper, and varnished (figure 69).

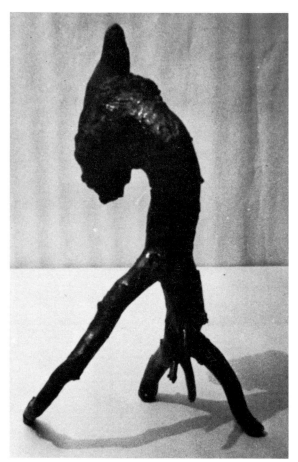

69 'Found' log sculpture

Prints and rubbings from wood

Interesting prints can be taken from engraved or impressed blocks of strawboard, hardboard, balsa wood or similar woods (figure 70). Blocks can also be made by gluing strips of balsa wood or matchsticks, to a hardboard base, see figure 29. Rubbings from wood grain can be used in collage and pictorial work, a practice known as *frottage*. The surrealist painter Max Ernst frequently employed this technique, making rubbings of floorboards and other wooden surfaces.

70 Rubbings from wood grain

55

Nails and screws

Nails and screws can be used to join wooden shapes or attach other materials to a wooden surface. They are also useful, as in figure 72, to decorate a wooden surface, or, as in figure 71, to create a design in their own right. Nails and screws are available in various types and sizes, something which can be exploited, as in *Vertebrate Configuration, 1963*. Small wire nails 25 mm (1 in.) are generally the most suitable for joining parts of a simple construction, though the length and type of nails will obviously need to relate to the thickness and types of material being used. Softwoods are easier to nail, making them good for work with children. Nailed constructions can look clumsy and crude. If possible the nails should appear as part of the design and therefore unobtrusive, as in figure 73. It may be possible to fasten the parts together in such a way that the nails do not show on the completed model. Aluminium alloy nails, panel pins, veneer pins, clasp nails, clout nails, tacks, brass chair nails and staples are among other useful types. With the dowel screw two pieces of wood can be attached with no visible means. There are special types of screws available for certain woods. Chipboard, for example, is best attached with special chipboard screws to avoid splitting. Other wood screws come in three basic types: countersunk, round head, and oval head.

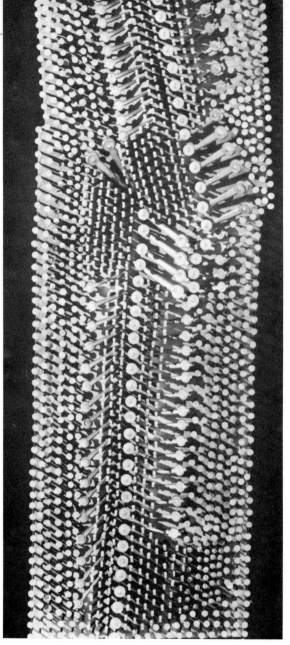

71 David Partridge, *Vertebrate Configuration, 1963* The Tate Gallery, London

72 Using nails

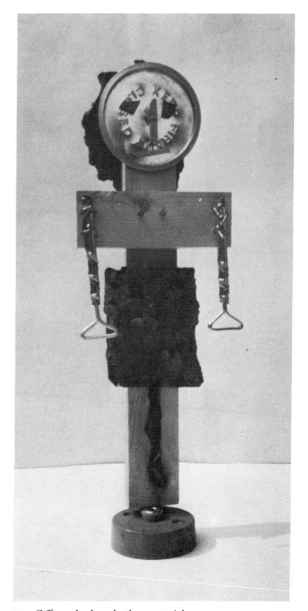

73 Offcuts, bark and other materials

6 Wire and metal

Models can be made from wire alone or by combining wire with other materials. Scrap metal can be glued or welded in various ways to form metal sculptures.

Lengths of soft aluminium wire of a reasonable gauge can be bent and twisted into shape. The pliable quality of this material means that it can be used by young children: it is a good material for simple, clean three-dimensional work. The direction of a bend can be altered without much ill effect, though persistent bending to and fro at the same point will, of course, create friction and an eventual break. Used in this way, wire may be likened to other modelling materials, for the character of a model can be rapidly changed simply by bending the wire with the fingers. Wire models might be considered as complete in themselves or they could be used as starting points or three-dimensional 'sketches' for larger and more complex work. As with clay, because forms are easily changed, an idea can quickly be developed.

Wire is obtainable in round and square section, aluminium, iron, brass and copper being the most common types. It is normally sold in coils, either by weight, for example 3 kg (7 lb), or by approximate length, 23 m (25 yd). For model and relief work various thicknesses could be used as well as a combination of different types. The gauge is similar to that of knitting needles: 20 g is fine, while 12 g cannot be bent smoothly by hand. 3 mm 3/32 in.) and 18 g aluminium wire is recommended. Plastic coated wire is also useful. For simple models a pair of wire cutters is the only necessary tool. Heavier wire can be shaped with pliers and can be hammered and flattened. Wire can be soldered and welded, either to other lengths of wire or to other metal shapes. It can, of course, be combined in various ways with paper, wood and other materials. One can print from wire blocks and make impressions and patterns from a small coil dipped in acrylic or other paint of thick consistency.

Starting with a single length of wire

Simple work could start with a single length of wire, perhaps an old coat-hanger or some wire saved from a packing case, which is twisted and bent into shape. In fact, without the aid of a soldering iron, joining lengths of wire is difficult and, unless integrated into the design, the joins often look crude and awkward. The 'twist' join is the neatest: overlap the two lengths of wire at right-angles to each other so that there is about 25 mm (1 in.) of overlap on each length, then use a pair of flat nose or combination pliers to twist the two ends together. Lengths can also be bound together with much thinner wire, such as florist wire or fuse wire. Plastic sticky tape can also be used. It is possible to match the colour of this with that of plastic-coated wire to achieve almost invisible joints. A resin glue, such as *Araldite* can also be used to join various wire shapes. The disadvantage here is that shapes normally have to be clamped in place for several hours while the glue dries.

Soft wire can be coiled round such things as pencils or tubing, as in figure 74. The wings of this model were made by pasting paper shapes over a wire support or armature.

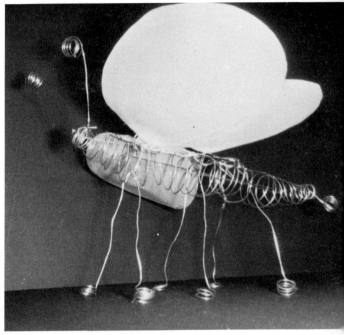

74 Coiled wire and paper

Welding and soldering techniques

Work which started by simply bending wire into interesting forms can be developed, by the introduction of heat, into more complex structures. The use of an oxy-acetylene welding blow-torch or a natural gas and compressed air brazing hearth torch will enable rods and metal shapes to be welded together, making possible work of greater permanence and variety.

The basis of all welding techniques is the use of heat, in fact the burning of the metals, so as to unite by fusion one part with another. The blacksmith's technique is to hammer the two parts together after heating them to the correct temperature. When welding iron or steel in this manner the pieces have to be brought to bright red heat. 'Spot-welding' and 'seam-welding' involve the direct application of heat with a welding torch so as to melt the metal and cause it, in its molten state, to infuse with that of the shape to which it is to be joined. 'Fusion welding' is an alternative method. Here, molten metal is poured into a joint so as partly to melt the two surfaces and so cause them to unite. Welding can also be done by the 'resistance butt' method, involving the use of an electric current, and the 'argon arc' process, as applied to aluminium.

Metals can also be joined by the insertion between them of an alloy of lower melting-point; this is known as soldering. Tin, copper, brass and zinc are usually joined with 'common' or 'soft' solder, which normally consists of lead and tin, with some antimony. A soldering-iron is used to melt the solder over the faces of the join. The iron may be heated in a reducing gas flame, or by electricity. The surfaces must be absolutely clean, otherwise the solder may fail to 'wet' them and so alloy itself to their surfaces. Surfaces should be treated with a flux such as zinc chloride or a resin to prevent oxidation when the hot solder is applied. 'Hard' solders, with a higher melting-point may be used to make stronger joins. Iron and steel are often soldered with brass containing 60 per cent zinc. Here, a blow-lamp or gas-torch is used to melt the brass, a process called 'brazing'.

All of these methods require special equipment and the use of a suitable studio or 'shop'. Such techniques can really only be learned from an expert, and under close supervision. As with all crafts, this requires a disciplined approach and, of course, there are technical limitations. This work can certainly be carried out in schools and it might be possible for more schools to develop part of their craft area to accommodate it. Metal sculpture is not an activity for large groups though, and the dangers of heat and fire do not need emphasizing. Anyone participating in this craft must be dressed correctly, wear protective goggles, and be thoroughly familiar with the equipment he is using.

Figure 75 shows an example of welding using round rod and sheet steel. This and the following three illustrations also suggest possibilities for the use of wire and scrap metal without welding.

It has been mentioned before that it can be advantageous to develop an idea first in the form of sketches. Ideas on paper can, however, be too imaginative and may fail to materialise because of the practical issues involved. Students should be made aware of technical processes and the limitations of the materials they will use. *Whirlwind*, for example, figure 76, was created from steel rod and formed into 50 mm (2 in.) diameter circles and then welded together. In figure 78 the design was developed from photographs in a Biology text book. The sculpture was made from steel tube, steel rod and welding rods. Other examples of metal sculpture can be seen in figures 92 to 95.

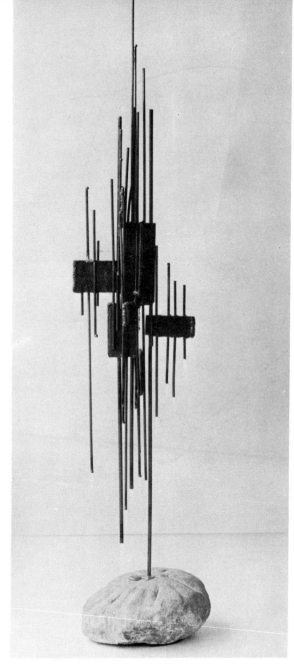

75 Welded rod and sheet steel: boy aged twelve

76 *Whirlwind*, steel rod: boy aged twelve

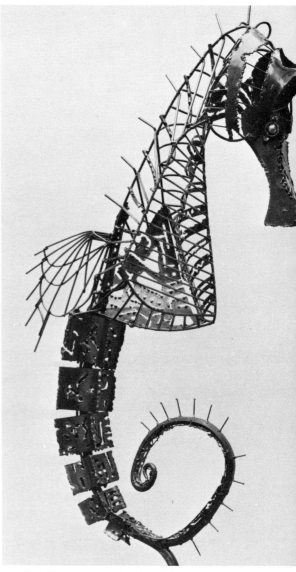

77 *Sea-Horse*, sheet steel and rod: boy aged seventeen
Selected by the Leicester Planning Department
for permanent exhibition in the city

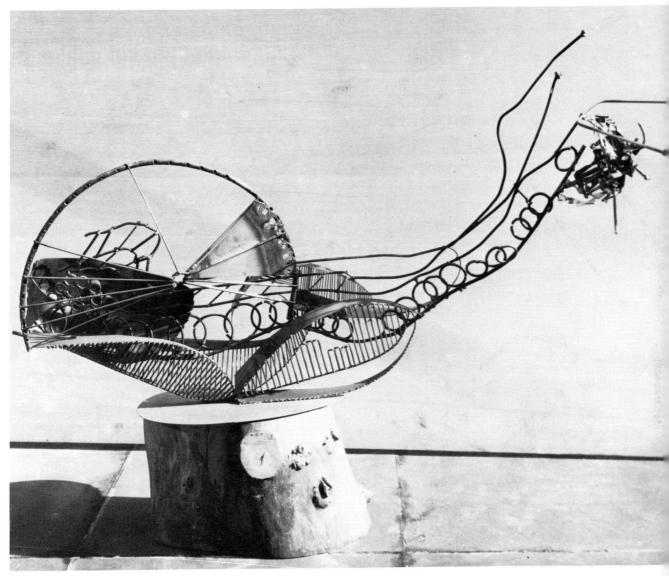

78 *Snail* 1.2 m × 0.75 m (48 in. × 30 in.)
steel and welding rods: boy aged sixteen

Wire mesh

As a basis for modelling with papier mâché or plaster, wire mesh is invaluable. Again there are various types and gauges; 12 mm ($\frac{1}{2}$ in.) mesh (chicken wire) is suitable for the work described here. This is easily fashioned into shape and forms a sturdy supporting structure for the application of plaster or pasted paper.

Masks may be made in this way. The method of working is illustrated in diagrammatic form in figure 80. The basic wire mesh shape is covered with strips of newspaper which have been pasted on one side with wallpaper adhesive. Mix the paste as instructed on the packet, usually one heaped teaspoonful per half pint. Apply the paste generously. Several layers of these newspaper strips are required; each layer should be applied in a different direction to that beneath it. The top layer can be one of white newsprint or similar thin paper. When completely dry (and this may take several days) the mask can be painted and varnished. Making masks is a favourite project with children of the nine to twelve age range. This work can be linked with the study of primitive masks and can involve the making of preliminary designs, as in figure 79. Masks can also be made from wood, paper and cardboard.

79 Design for a mask

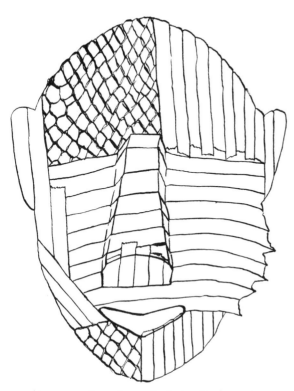

80 Diagram to show the method of making a papier
mâché mask

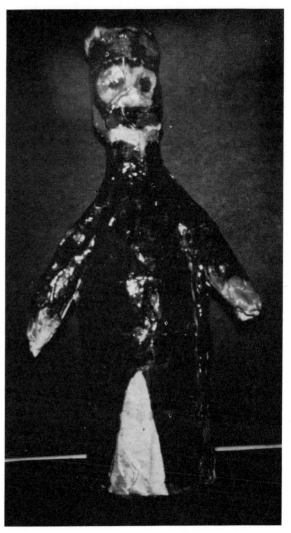

81 Papier mâché built around a bottle: boy aged nine

Other models can be made in a similar way by applying strips of pasted paper around other objects, even around some screwed-up newspaper. The use of wallpaper paste also acts as a size, strengthening the paper and rendering it less porous. Generous pasting is necessary. In figure 81 the model was built up over a bottle.

Wire armatures

Wire, perhaps combined with wire mesh, can be used in the construction of armatures for sculpture. See figure 83. The wire or metal support is vital in work involving plaster of paris, cement, or *Poly-filla* (*Spackle*). The armature forms the basic shape of the work, acting as a foundation on which to build. With large scale work the armature may necessarily become quite complex, whilst with simple models it could consist merely of a single strand of wire attached with wire staples to a wooden base. In making the armature one must bear in mind that it is going to be supporting a certain weight of plaster, cement or other material and it must therefore be securely attached to a base block.

Plaster does not readily stick to a metal surface and it is therefore necessary to coat the armature with a layer of scrim or newspaper. This is used as described above, torn into strips and wrapped around the wire structure. Strips of fabric offcuts or waste, such as cotton, can be used, but avoid heavy fabric. The paper can be held in place with a few touches of glue, whilst a little plaster will hold scrim and fabric. Most models will, in any case, need padding out in this way as it is both undesirable and uneconomical to create the full thickness of the shape simply by using plaster. Thick plaster is likely to crack.

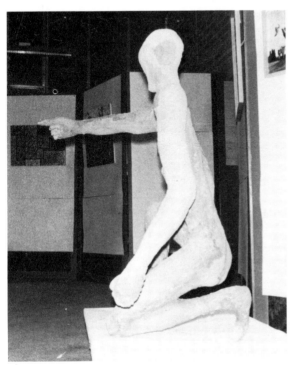

82 *Figure*, cement: boy aged seventeen

83 Diagram to illustrate the construction of an armature

Plaster, *Polyfilla* (*Spackle*) or cement can then be applied over such a foundation. This should be done little by little, using a wet knife, modelling tool or trowel. Keeping the tool wet will help with the modelling and produce a smoother finish. Plaster which is incorrectly mixed or has become too wet will run and be impossible to work. Particularly with craft *Polyfilla*, it is possible to build the model up in a number of layers, allowing each to dry before the next is added. Keep to thin coatings of plaster and cement, as there is a tendency for these materials to crack if they reach any depth. The work must be allowed to dry in an even temperature and away from draught. Failure to do this can also result in cracking.

Finished dry work can be modified or smoothed down with abrasive paper. It can be painted, though some people prefer a natural finish.

Wire and plaster figures

The wire, paper, plaster method is ideal for figures and may be used as an introduction to sculpture. It is possible to do this as classwork; successful results can be achieved with twelve year olds. However, as with all work involving construction, it would be impossible in the average art room and with a large class for each member to make his own armature. It is suggested that the rough armatures, consisting of one or two strands of wire fixed to an offcut of wood are made beforehand by the teacher. The pupil is then able to bend the wire to form an individual armature on which to work.

The work of a number of modern as well as primitive artists may be used as inspiration; see, for example, the *Man Pointing* by Alberto Giacometti. Sculptures such as this are usually made in plaster before being cast in bronze. Like similar sculptures by Giacometti, the gesture is important in involving the spectator with the sculpture. It is a work which exemplifies the qualities of a good piece of sculpture. It says just enough, it works within the technical limitations of the art, it is simple, powerful, expressive. Themes such as those used by Giacometti, *Man Pointing, Walking Man, Standing Woman* and so on, make interesting starting points. The over-riding aim should be the creation of something which is visually powerful.

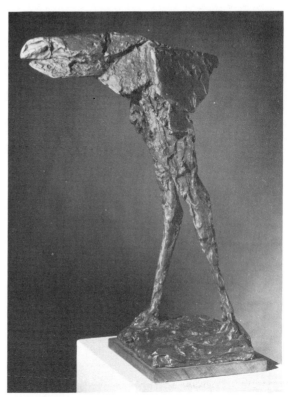

85 Elizabeth Frink, *Harbinger Bird*
The Tate Gallery, London

84 Alberto Giacometti, *Man Pointing*
The Tate Gallery, London

This may be achieved by stance, interplay of shapes, textures or colours, or perhaps a combination of two or more of these qualities. As with all art it may be necessary to exaggerate or distort in order to obtain the desired effect.

An example by a first year Advanced Level student is shown in figures 86 and 87. The armature here was made from wire mesh coated with scrim and then plaster. The model was developed from the study of bone shapes.

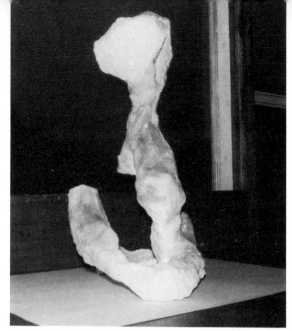

86 Plaster over wire mesh: boy aged sixteen

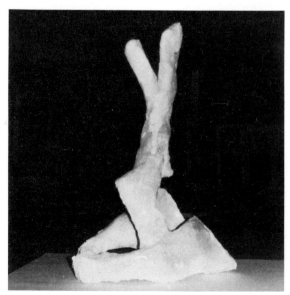

87 Plaster over wire mesh: boy aged sixteen

Junk sculpture

'Junk' sculpture has really evolved since the first 'ready-made' of Marcel Duchamp. Other modern artists, among them Picasso, have taken discarded metal items and welded them together in a sort of three-dimensional collage. This can be done in a modest way with the waste metal products of the home, for example, tin cans, lids, parts of an old clock and so on. This type of work can be developed further and on a larger scale, involving the techniques of welding and soldering. However, the aim of this book is to keep the scope of the work within the capabilities of the non-specialist, and common metal waste can be assembled and attached by gluing, or may perhaps be nailed or wired together. The choice of method will largely depend on the materials used.

In any case, junk sculpture is probably more for the individual than being in the normal run of classwork. It involves the same problems as collage in that the selection and relation of objects must in some way be meaningful. It should be more than just an attractive assemblage of rubbish.

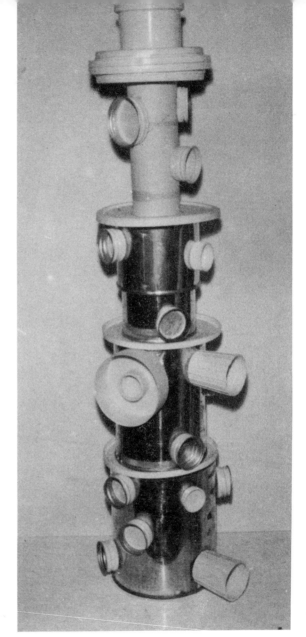

88   Tins and lids

71

Further examples of metal sculpture appear in figures 92 to 95. The inspiration for figure 92 came from exploring a metal scrapyard. The student discovered a distinctive piece of solid copper anode that had been used in electroplating. Some additional shaping and other work, emphasizing the scaly texture, produced an immensely satisfying form which is mounted on a polished slate base.

89 Chessmen from found materials: boy aged fourteen

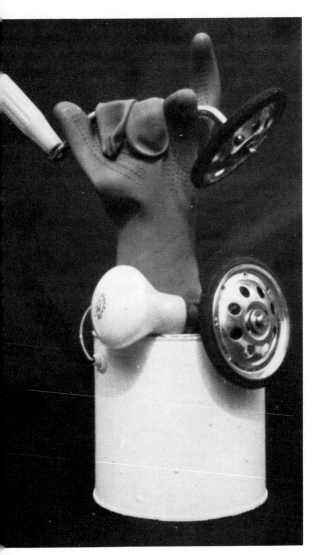

91 Various materials

90 'Junk' sculpture

73

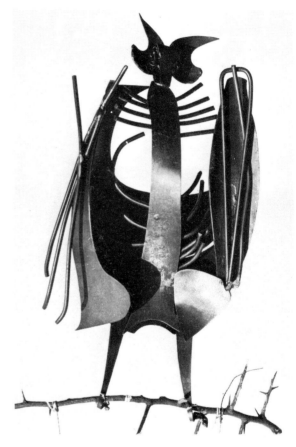

93 *Bat*, sheet steel and round steel rods: boy aged seventeen

92 Copper anode: boy aged sixteen

74

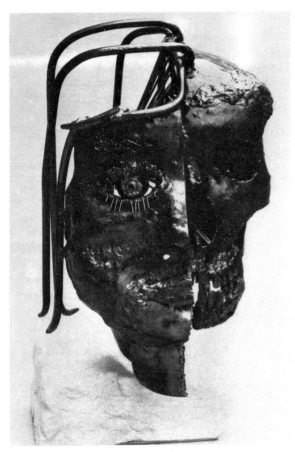

94 *Head*, sheet and round rod mild steel:
boy aged seventeen

95 *Horse and Jockey*
Sheet and round rod mild steel: boy aged seventeen

7 Other ideas

The previous sections have considered common waste materials and suggested ways in which these might be used. Most of these materials will be available at home and in school, whilst sources for the more unusual scrap have been mentioned in section 2. Most readers will wish to go beyond many of the obvious suggestions and techniques.

Inevitably in a book which attempts to deal with such a huge subject a particular idea can only be touched on. There are all sorts of ways, for example, of using polystyrene waste, or designing with pieces of string, or making mosaics with egg shells. There is not space to deal with every aspect of such topics, and it must therefore be left to the reader to probe further as well as to seek information from specialized books. I conclude by illustrating and listing a number of other ideas which do not relate directly to the previous text.

Polystyrene

The polystyrene model shown in figure 97 was made from shapes used as packaging material glued together with *Copydex*. Polystyrene can also be glued with PVA medium, though the glue tends to take rather longer to dry. Polystyrene is frequently used as protective packaging for household goods, and offcuts from ceiling tiles may also be available. It varies in thickness and texture, and sometimes has an impressed design or pattern, or is moulded to a particular shape, as in the illustration. Polystyrene is best cut with a hot wire. A length of thin wire heated through a candle flame is adequate, or one can obtain an electric or battery-operated hot wire cutter. The former method has obvious hazards, if misused, and could be a potential fire risk, especially when used by children. I mention though that I have used this method successfully with children of twelve years old. Polystyrene is easily painted with craft paint, which makes it useful for relief work. Shapes can be impressed into its surface, and blocks so treated can be used to obtain rubbings and prints.

96 Polystyrene waste

97 Polystyrene waste

Nature

Nature is an excellent source of interesting scrap, see section 2. Leaves, for instance, can be used in collage form, painted with poster or powder paint for impressed work as in figure 100, or used for offset or direct prints. Mosaic work, similar to the paper mosaics illustrated in figures 19 and 20, can be achieved by impressing a variety of small shells and pebbles into wet plaster. Egg shells are also useful for this technique: they can be dyed different colours before being broken up into suitable pieces. Egg shell can also be glued to a paper or cardboard support, as in figure 102, which also makes use of feathers. Large pebbles can be painted and varnished, a technique which will probably best suit younger children, though sophisticated results in the manner of Brancusi's sculpture (figure 103) can be achieved. Local stone can often be carved, provided chisels and other necessary tools are available (figure 98). One or two other examples involving natural materials are shown in the following illustrations.

98 Drilled slate

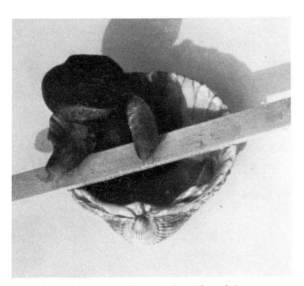

99 *Man in a boat*, natural materials: girl aged six

100 Leaf prints

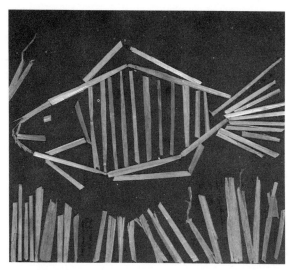

101 Straw

102 Feathers, egg shell

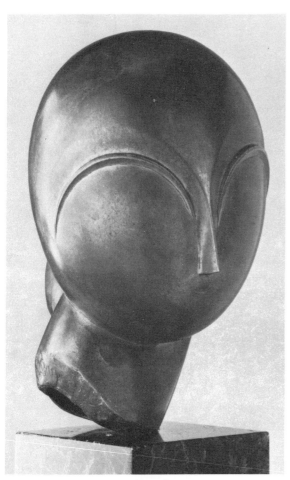

103 Constantin Brancusi, *Danaide*
The Tate Gallery, London

104 Various materials

Glass

Figure 105 shows a design made from glass. The work consists of hundreds of small fragments of coloured glass glued to a painted hardboard support. Much of the glass was obtained from broken bottles. This is a hazardous technique but one which can produce very effective results.

105 Glass chippings: boy aged fifteen

Perspex

Perspex waste was used in figure 106 combined with thread.

Marion Richardson once said that 'A factor of great importance is the interest of the children'. The use of different, unusual materials could be one way of arousing interest. The twentieth century has found the artist searching wider than ever before, discovering and examining new materials and new techniques. Stimulation has come from the East, from tribal carvings of primitive Africa as well as from the sophisticated abstracts, brash pop paintings or involved Kinetic works of the present day. The teacher and the individual should look at as many different art forms as possible. The more one looks the more one sees, the more one sees the wider becomes one's visual knowledge and vocabulary. This book considers some new ways of looking at scrap and common rubbish. I hope the reader will have been stimulated enough to go beyond the last page and to be constantly aware of art in the widest sense, feeding his mind with new ideas and fresh information.

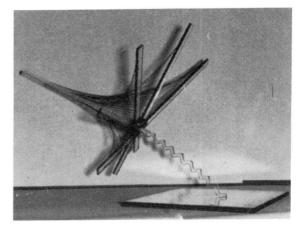

106 Perspex and thread: boy aged fifteen

8 Technical notes

Detailed information relating to materials, methods and equipment will be found in appropriate parts of the text. The notes that follow summarise ways of finishing the basic work and of displaying it.

Painting

Most three-dimensional work can be painted. The paint is selected according to its suitability for a particular surface or material. The work can be brush painted or sprayed with a spray diffuser, a spray gun or aerosol cans of paint. Other painting techniques such as flicking and splattering can also be used. Powder paint, poster paint and emulsion paints tend to suit cardboard and paper surfaces, whilst gloss and enamel paints are better for glass, plastics and metals. Acrylic and PVA paints can also be used as glue. *Reeves Craft Paint* is suitable for all types of work, including printmaking. If the model is placed on some sheets of newspaper before it is painted, this will make cleaning up easier, as the paper is simply thrown away. Gloss, enamel and some spray paints will require turpentine substitute for cleaning up and rinsing brushes; other paints are easily diluted in either hot or cold water and these are recommended for use with children.

Staining and varnishing

Various stains are obtainable for use on wood, as are gloss and matt varnishes. Clear varnishes are now available for most surfaces, and a construction which is to stand out-of-doors should be treated in this way. The varnish may be applied with a soft, clean brush or sprayed from an aerosol can. PVA medium thinned with water can be used as a varnish over collage work or on paper and cardboard models. Paper varnish, *Cryla No 1 Gloss Medium*, *Cryla No 2 Matt Medium*, and *Marvin Medium* are also useful.

Texturing

Papier mâché, cardboard and similar surfaces can be textured by painting them with plaster or *Polyfilla*. Wood surfaces can be roughened with a rasp or coarse sandpaper. Fine sandpaper is useful for smoothing sawn edges.

Overworking

This technique is particularly suitable for collage work, which can be overworked by employing various graphic techniques, or by fumage or décollage. Prints can be overprinted; various methods are suggested in the text.

Fixing

Graphic work done in pencil, chalk or crayons may require an application of fixative to prevent it smudging. Fixative is obtainable in aerosol cans or may be applied from a bottle, using a spray diffuser. Prints can also be fixed in this way.

Drying

Glued work must be allowed to dry completely before it is moved or painted. The storage of such work must therefore be considered. Similarly, painted work must be dry before it is varnished. Varnish and paint applied from aerosol cans must be allowed to dry before further coats are added. Prints must be properly dry before they are stored or mounted for display. They may be left on a flat surface, pinned through one corner to a display board, or suspended from a 'drying-line'. A 'drying-line' or rack can be made by threading a length of string or a length cut from an old washing line through bulldog clips and fixing this fairly high up across the room so that it is taut. Prints may then be suspended from the bulldog clips.

Mounting and presentation

Prints, collage and graphic work must be dry and may need trimming. Mounts are best made from thick card of a neutral colour. They should be cut to a size which allows for a slight border around the work, between the work and the mount. Mounts may be framed under glass. Models and constructions often benefit from a small base. A block of painted, varnished or natural wood is normally adequate. Any form of mounting should aim to enhance the result of the finished work rather than detract from it.

9 Further reading

Carton Craft, Richard Slade, Faber, London
Creative Corrugated Paper Craft, Rolf Hartung, Batsford, London
Collage and Found Art, Dona Meilach and Elvie Ten Hoor, Allen and Unwin, London; Crown, New York
Sculpture in Paper, Ralph Fabri, Watson-Guptill, New York
Creative Paper Craft, Ernst Röttger, Batsford, London; Van Nostrand Reinhold, New York
Take an Egg Box, Richard Slade, Faber, London
Papier Mâché Artistry, Dona Meilach, Allen and Unwin, London; Crown, New York
Max Ernst Frottages, Werner Spies, Thames and Hudson, London
Introducing Fabric Collage, Margaret Connor, Batsford, London; Watson-Guptill, New York
Designing with String, Mary Seyd, Batsford, London; Watson-Guptill, New York
Introducing Seed Collage, Caryl and Gordon Simms, Batsford, London; Watson-Guptill, New York
Art from Found Materials, Mary Lou Stribling, Allen and Unwin, London; Crown, New York
Found by Chance, Lothar Kampmann, Evans, London
Paper Straw Craft, Anne Stone, Mills and Boon, London; Sterling, New York
Frontiers of Printmaking, Michael Rothenstein, Studio Vista, London
Introducing Abstract Printmaking, Robin Capon, Batsford, London; Watson-Guptill, New York
A Concise History of Modern Sculpture, Herbert Read, Thames and Hudson, London; Praeger, New York
Picasso Sculpture; A Complete Catalogue, Werner Spies, Thames and Hudson, London; Abrams, New York
Picasso: Sculpture, Ceramics, Graphic Work, Arts Council 1967
Direct Metal Sculpture, Dona Meilach and Don Seiden, Allen and Unwin, London; Crown, New York
Creative Metal Craft, Heinz Ullrich and Dieter Klante, Batsford, London
Simple Wire Sculpture, Elizabeth Gallop, Studio Vista, London; Watson-Guptill, New York
Fun with Junk, Sawako Goda, Whiting and Wheaton, London
Creative Woodcraft, Ernst Röttger, Batsford, London; Van Nostrand Reinhold, New York